The Ladybird Key Words Reading Scheme is based on these commonly used words. Those used most often in the English language are introduced first—with other words of popular appeal to children. All the Key Words list is covered in the early books, and the later titles use further word lists to develop full reading fluency. The total number of different words which will be learned in the complete reading scheme is nearly two thousand. The gradual introduction of these words, frequent repetition and complete 'carry-over' from book to book, will ensure rapid learning.

The full-colour illustrations have been designed to create a desirable attitude towards learning—by making every child *eager* to read each title. Thus this attractive reading scheme embraces not only the latest findings in word frequency, but also the natural interests and activities of happy children.

Each book contains a list of the new words introduced.

W. MURRAY, t'   ·rds
Reading Schem   hor
and lecturer on   10r,
with J. McNall\   er's
book published   td.

D1327029

THE LADYBIRD KEY WORDS READING SCHEME has 12 graded books in each of its three series—'a', 'b' and 'c'. As explained in the handbook 'Teaching Reading', these 36 graded books are all written on a controlled vocabulary, and take the learner from the earliest stages of reading to reading fluency.

The 'a' series gradually introduces and repeats new words. The parallel 'b' series gives the needed further repetition of these words at each stage, but in different context and with different illustrations.

The 'c' series is also parallel to the 'a' series, and supplies the necessary link with writing and phonic training.

An illustrated booklet—'Notes for Teachers'—can be obtained free from the publishers. This booklet fully explains the Key Words principle and the Ladybird Key Words Reading Scheme. It also includes information on the reading books, work books and apparatus available, and such details as the vocabulary loading and reading ages of all books.

BOOK 4a
The Ladybird Key Words Reading Scheme

Things we do

by W. MURRAY
with illustrations by J. H. WINGFIELD

Publishers: Ladybird Books Ltd . Loughborough
© Ladybird Books Ltd (formerly Wills & Hepworth Ltd) 1964
Printed in England

Peter and Jane are at home.

Peter wants to make a car to play with. He wants to make a car like Daddy's.

Jane looks on. "It is good," she says, "we can have fun with it."

"I want to make it red," says Peter.

"Yes," says Jane, "make it red. You and I like red."

---

new words

make   she

Jane likes to help Mummy. She wants to make cakes like Mummy.

"Let me help you, Mummy," she says. "Will you let me help, please? I can make cakes like you."

"Yes," says Mummy, "I will let you help me. You are a good girl."

"We will make some cakes for Peter and Daddy," says Jane. "They like the cakes we make."

---

new words

let   will

Peter and Jane like to draw. "Let us draw," says Jane. "I will draw you, Peter," she says.

"Yes, let us draw," says Peter. "I will draw a tree."

"Here you are, Peter," says Jane. "Here is Pat, and here is a ball. I will make the ball red. Come and look, Peter, come and look at this dog."

---

new words

draw   us

"I will draw," says Peter. "I like to draw. Look, Jane, look at this tree," he says. "I will draw a house in the tree. See this house."

"Let us make a house in a tree, Jane," says Peter. "Will Daddy let us? Will he let us make a house in a tree?"

"Yes, Peter," she says, "he will help us make it."

---

new word

house

Daddy lets the children have a house in a tree. He draws the house, and helps the children make it.

"It will be a good house," says Peter. "It will be a good house for us to play in."

"Yes," says Jane, "it will be fun to play in it. Look, Pat wants to come up with us."

---

new words

children   be

The children are in the house in the tree. The dog is with the children.

"Let us have tea here," says Jane. "That will be fun," she says.

"Yes," says Peter, "you make the tea. I will draw. I will draw some flowers."

"Yes, I will be like Mummy and get the tea," says Jane. "I like to get the tea."

no new words

The children are on the bus. Pat is with the children. He wants to jump up with Jane.

"No," says Jane to the dog. "Get off, Pat. Get off. Be a good dog."

"Look," says Peter, "there go the Police. There is a Police car. Can you see, Jane? There they go."

"Yes," says Jane. "Here are the shops," she says. "Let us get off here."

---

new words

off   there

The children get off the bus, then they go off to the shops for Mummy.

" Let us shop for Mummy, then we can look at the sweets and toys," says Jane.

"There is the fish shop," she says, " we have to get fish."

"Yes," says Peter. "You get the fish. I will get apples and cakes."

The children go into the shops.

---

new word

then

The children are at home. They make a shop. "I will be the man in the shop," says Peter.

"Then let me be Mummy," Jane says. "I want some things for the house," she says, "and then I want some things for tea. Give me some flowers, please, and I want some apples."

Peter puts in the flowers and the apples. "There you are," he says.

---

new words

things   puts

The children have to work.

Peter has to help Daddy work with the car. Jane has to help Mummy work in the house. She likes to help Mummy work.

"It is good to work, and it is good to play," says Mummy. "Let us put the play things away, and then water the flowers. Then we will make the beds," she says.

---

new words

work   away

Peter is at work with his daddy. He likes to work with his daddy.

"Go away," he says to Pat, "go away. Be off. Be off, I want to work."

Daddy says, "Put the things down there, and then help me make a fire."

Peter puts his things down. "Good," he says, "I want to make a fire."

---

new words

his   fire

Peter helps his Daddy to make a big fire.

"I like this work," says Peter.

"It is like play," says Jane. "Put some things on the fire, Daddy wants a big fire."

"Yes," says Daddy, "make a big fire. Keep the dog away. Keep Pat away."

"Come here, Pat," says Jane, "come to me. Be a good dog and keep away."

---

new words

big   keep

You can see Daddy at his big fire.

The children like to play with water. Jane has a big boat and Peter has a little boat. Pat wants to play with Peter's little boat.

"Keep Pat away," says Peter to Jane. "He wants my boat. He wants my little boat."

"Come here, Pat," says Jane. "You can have my ball to play with."

---

new words

little   my

The two children are in the water. They want to fish.

Peter has a fish. "Look at my big one," he says.

"Will you keep it?" says Jane.

"No," he says. Peter puts his big fish into the water.

Jane says, "Look, I have two little ones." She puts her fish into the water. She puts her two little ones in.

"Off they go," Jane says.

---

new words

two   her

The two children are at the farm. They want to help at the farm. They like to work there.

Here they are with the horses.

Jane likes her little horse. She gives it an apple. She wants to keep her little horse.

Peter has a big horse. "I want to get on my horse, Jane," he says. "Help me up please."

---

new words

farm   horse

Jane helps Peter to get on his big horse. "There you are," she says, "away you go."

"Thank you," says Peter. "Thank you, Jane."

Then Jane gets on her little horse. "Away I go, on my horse," she says.

The two children go off to work on the farm.

"Let us help with the cows," says Peter. "Yes," says Jane, "we will help with the cows."

---

new words

thank   cows

" Let us help the man milk the cows," says Jane. "Will he let us help him milk?" she says.

" Yes," says Peter, "he likes us to help him with his work."

" Can we help you?" says Peter.

" Thank you," says the man. " Yes, please. You two can help me with the milk. Put the horses away. Come in and help me with the cows."

---

new words

milk   him.

The two children play at home.

"What will you do?" says Jane. "I will make a toy farm," Peter says. "What will you do, Jane?"

"I want to help you make the farm," she says. "Thank you," says Peter.

"The farm house was there," he says. "Here is the little horse and my big horse. Let the man milk his cows. Keep the dog away. Put him with the horses."

---

new words

what   do

Jane likes cats. She has a little cat.

"What do you want?" she says to her cat. "Do you want some milk?"

"The cows on the farm give good milk," says Jane. "I will give him some."

Peter comes in with his big rabbit. "What is that, Jane?" he says. "Is it milk? Give some to my rabbit, please."

"Thank you," he says. "Keep the cat away."

---

new word

cat

The children, Daddy and Mummy all go to the sea. Here they all are in the train at the station.

The cat and the dog are at home.

Peter says, "Away we all go to the sea. What can we do at the sea, Daddy?"

"You can all do what you like," Daddy says to him.

"Thank you," says Peter. "I will go into the water."

---

new words

all   sea

Here they all are at the sea. The children can do what they like. They can go into the sea, play games, or fish, or be with Mummy and Daddy.

"Play a game with us, Daddy," says Peter. "Yes, play a game, please," says Jane.

Daddy says he will play a game with the big red ball.

"Good," says Jane, "it is fun to play games with him."

---

new words

game   or

The two children like to play games. The cat looks on.

Peter says, "Do you want to play with my toys or play at schools?"

"Let us play at schools," says Jane. "What will you do, read or draw?"

"I want to read," says Peter. "All children like to read."

"Read this," says Jane. "Read this, Peter."

Peter reads. "It says DANGER," he says. "I can read DANGER."

"Yes, it is DANGER," Jane says.

---

new words

read   DANGER

Jane's cat is not big. She likes to go up the tree for a game.

"Stop her," says Jane, "she gets up the tree and can not get down. Stop her, Peter. Please stop her."

Peter can not stop the cat. "She can not get down," he says. "There is no danger. You or I can get her, or we can get Daddy to help."

"No," says Jane, "all we have to do is get some milk."

The cat sees the milk and then comes down.

---

new words

not   stop

Daddy, Mummy, Jane, Peter and Pat are all here. The cat is at home.

"Look," says Peter, "there is DANGER, STOP. I can read DANGER, STOP."

Jane says, "I can read TO THE SEA and TO THE STATION."

Daddy says, "Yes, that is good. You can read."

Jane says to Pat, "Come here. You are not to jump up at the car. It is not Daddy's car."

"Let us all go home to tea," says Mummy.

"Yes," says Daddy, "we will all go home."

New words used in this book

Page		
4	make	she
6	let	will
8	draw	us
10	house	
12	children	be
14	—	
16	off	there
18	then	
20	things	puts
22	work	away
24	his	fire
26	big	keep

Page		
28	little	my
30	two	her
32	farm	horse
34	thank	cows
36	milk	him
38	what	do
40	cat	
42	all	sea
44	game	or
46	read DANGER	
48	not	stop
50	—	

Total number of new words 41